How to Raise Your Credit Score Fast

And Get out of Debt

Author Logan Hill

Copyright © 2018 by Logan Hill. All Right Reserved.

No part of this publication may be reproduced, distributed, or transmitted in any form or by any means, including photocopying, recording, or other electronic or mechanical methods, or by any information storage and retrieval system without the prior written permission of Smith Show Publishing, except in the case of very brief quotations embodied in critical reviews and certain other noncommercial uses permitted by copyright law.

How to Raise Your Credit Score

What is a credit report?..2

Why should i check my credit report?..........................3

How do i get my credit report?......................................3

How do i correct errors on my credit report?...........4

How long can negative information stay on my credit report?..5

How can my credit report affect my job application?......10

What is a credit freeze?...11

What is a fraud alert?...14

What is a credit score?...16

What are my options for dealing with debt?......................21

Got bad credit?
Steer clear of credit repair scams..22

What is a credit report?

A credit report includes information on where you live, how you pay your bills, and whether you've been sued or have filed for bankruptcy. Nationwide credit reporting companies sell the information in your report to creditors, insurers, employers, and other businesses that, in turn, use it to evaluate your applications for credit, insurance, employment, or renting a place to live.

Why should I check my credit report?

Some financial advisors and consumer advocates suggest that you review your credit report several times a year. Why?

- the information in it affects whether you can get a loan—and how much you will have to pay to borrow money.

- to make sure the information is accurate, complete, and up-to-date before you apply for a loan for a major purchase like a house or car, buy insurance, or apply for a job.

- to help repair possible identity theft. identity thieves may use your information to open new credit accounts in your name.
then, when they don't pay the bills, the delinquent account is reported on your credit report. inaccurate information like that could affect your ability to get credit, insurance, or even a job.

How do I get my credit report?

By law, you're entitled to a free copy of your credit report from each of the nationwide credit reporting companies —equifax, experian, and transUnion —once every 12 months. to order, visit **annualcreditreport.com** or call 1-877-322-8228.

You may order reports from one, two, or all three of the companies at the same time, or you may stagger your requests. Some financial advisors say staggering your requests during a 12-month period may be a good way to keep an eye on the accuracy and completeness of the information in your reports. if you're getting ready to apply for a loan or job, you might want to check all three reports at the same time.

How do I correct errors on my credit report?

Both the credit reporting company and the information provider (that is, the person, company, or organization that provides information about you to a credit reporting company) are responsible for correcting inaccurate or incomplete information in your report once you bring it to their attention. Letting them know involves two steps:

Step One:

Tell the credit reporting company, in writing, what information you think is inaccurate. Your letter should identify each item in your report you dispute, explain why you dispute the information, and ask that it be removed or corrected. include copies (not originals) of documents that support your position. You may want to enclose a copy of your report with the items in question circled. Send your letter by certified mail, "return receipt requested," so you can document what the credit reporting company received. Keep copies of your dispute letter and enclosures.

Credit reporting companies must investigate the items in question usually within 30 days, unless they consider your dispute frivolous. they also must forward all the relevant data you provide about the inaccuracy to the information provider, which reviews the relevant information, investigates, and reports the results back to the credit reporting company. if the information provider finds the disputed information is inaccurate, it must notify all three nationwide credit reporting companies so they can correct the information in your file.

What happens after the investigation?

When the investigation is complete, the credit reporting company must give you the results in writing and a free copy of your report if the dispute results in a change. if an item is changed or deleted, the credit reporting company cannot put the disputed information back in your file unless the information provider verifies that it is accurate and complete. the credit reporting company also must send you written notice that includes the name, address, and phone number of the information provider.

if you ask, the credit reporting company must send notices of any corrections to anyone who received your report in the past six months. You can have a corrected copy of your report sent to anyone who received a copy during the past two years for employment purposes.

What if the investigation doesn't resolve my dispute?

Ask that a statement of the dispute be included in your file and in future reports. You also can ask the credit reporting company to provide your statement to anyone who received a copy of your report in the recent past. expect to pay a fee for this service.

Step Two

Tell the information provider, in writing, that you dispute an item in your credit report.

A sample dispute letter is included in this book. include copies (not originals) of documents that support your position. if the provider listed an address on your credit report, send your letter to that address. if no address is listed, contact the provider and ask for the correct address to send your letter. if the information provider does not give you an address, you can send your letter to any business

What if the provider continues to report the disputed item to a credit reporting company?

the provider must let the credit reporting company know about your dispute. And if you are correct —that is, if the information you dispute is found to be inaccurate or incomplete —the information provider must tell the credit reporting company to update or delete the item.

How long can negative information stay on my credit report?

A credit reporting company can report most accurate negative information for seven years and bankruptcy information for 10 years. there is no time limit on reporting information about criminal convictions; information reported in response to your application for a job that pays more than $75,000 a year; and information reported because you've applied for more than $150,000 worth of credit or life insurance. information about a lawsuit or an unpaid judgment against you can be reported for seven years or until the statute of limitations runs out, whichever is longer. the standard method for calculating the seven-year reporting period starts with the date that the event took place.

How can my credit report affect my job application?

When you apply for a job, employers look at the application you complete and the resume you prepare. Some employers also check into your background before they hire you. depending on the employer and the job, that background information might include your employment history, your driving record, criminal records, and your credit report.

days of learning the bad news.

An employer must get your permission before asking for a report about you from a credit reporting company or any other company that provides background information. if you don't give your okay, your application for employment may not get a second look. that's up to you. But if you don't get the job because of information in your report, the employer has some legal obligations: First, the employer must show you the report; second, the employer must tell you how to get your own copy. the report is free if you ask for it within 60 days of learning the bad news.

What is a credit freeze?

A credit freeze, also known as a security freeze, lets you restrict access to your credit report, which in turn makes it more difficult for identity thieves to open new accounts in your name. that's because most creditors need to look at your credit reportbefore approving a new account. if they can't see your file, they may not extend the credit.

You may want to place a credit freeze on your credit reports if you're concerned about the potential consequences of data breaches.

to place a freeze on your credit reports, contact each of the nationwide credit reporting companies:

Equifax —1-800-525-6285; equifax.com

Experian —1-888-397-3742; experian.com

TransUnion —1-800-680-7289; transunion.com

You'll need to supply your name, address, date of birth, Social Security number and other personal information. Fees vary based on where you live; they commonly range from $5 to $10.

A credit freeze does not:

- affect your credit score

- prevent you from getting your free annual credit report
- keep you from opening a new account, applying for a job, renting an apartment, or buying insurance. if you're doing any of these, you'll need to lift the freeze temporarily, either for a specific time, or for a specific party, say, a potential landlord or employer. the cost and lead times to lift a freeze vary, so it's best to check with the credit reporting company inadvance.

- prevent a thief from incurring charges on your existing accounts. You still need to monitor all bank, credit card and insurance statements for fraudulent transactions.

What is a fraud alert?

Unlike a credit freeze that locks down your credit, a fraud alert allows creditors to get a copy of your credit report as long as they take steps to verify your identity. For example, if you provide a telephone number, the business must call you to verify whether you are the person making the credit request. Fraud alerts may be effective at stopping someone from opening new credit accounts in your name, but they may not prevent the misuse of your existing accounts. You still need to monitor all bank, credit card and insurance statements for fraudulent transactions.

Initial Fraud Alert

if you're concerned about identity theft, but haven't yet become a victim, this fraud alert protects your credit from unverified access for at least 90 days. You may want to place a fraud alert on your file if your wallet, Social Security card, or other personal, financial or account information are ever lost or stolen.

Extended Fraud Alert

For victims of identity theft, an extended fraud alert protects your credit for seven years.

Active Duty Military Alert

For those in the military who want to protect their credit while deployed, this type of fraud alert lasts for one year.

to place a fraud alert on your credit reports, contact one of the nationwide credit reporting companies. A fraud alert is free. You must provide proof of your identity. the company you call must tell the other companies; they, in turn, will place an alert on their versions of your report.

What is a credit score?

credit scoring is a system creditors use to help determine whether to give you credit. it also may be used to help decide the credit terms you are offered or the rate you will pay for the loan.

information about you and your credit experiences, like your bill- paying history, the number and type of accounts you have, whether you pay your bills by the date they're due, collection actions, outstanding debt, and the age of your accounts, is collected from your credit report. Using a statistical program, creditors compare this information to the loan repayment history of consumers with similar profiles.

For example, a credit scoring system awards points for each factor that helps predict who is most likely to repay a debt. the total number of points —a credit score —helps predict how creditworthy you are: how likely it is that you will repay a loan and make the payments when they're due. A higher credit score is taken to mean you are less of a risk, which, in turn, means you are more likely to get credit or insurance — or pay less for it.

What factors affect my credit score?

credit scoring systems are complex and vary among creditors or insurance companies and for different types of credit or insurance. if one factor changes, your score may change —but improvement generally depends on how that factor relates to others the system considers. Only the business using the system knows what might improve your score under the particular model they use to evaluate your application.

Nevertheless, scoring models usually consider the following types of information in your credit report to help compute your credit score:

Have you paid your bills on time?

You can count on payment history to be a significant factor. if your credit report indicates that you have paid bills late, had an account referred to collections, or declared bankruptcy, it is likely to have a negative effect on your score.

Are you maxed out?

Many scoring systems evaluate the amount of debt you have compared to your credit limits. if the amount you owe is close to your credit limit, it's likely to have a negative effect on your score.

How long have you had credit?

Generally, scoring systems consider your credit track record. An insufficient credit history may affect your score negatively, but factors like timely payments and low balances can offset that.

Have you applied for new credit lately?

Many scoring systems consider whether you have applied for credit recently by looking at "inquiries" on your credit report. if you have applied for too many new accounts recently, it could have a negative effect on your score. every inquiry isn't counted: for example, inquiries by creditors who are monitoring your account or looking at credit reports to make "prescreened" credit offers are not considered liabilities.

How many credit accounts do you have and what kinds of accounts are they?

Although it is generally considered a plus to have established credit accounts, too many credit card accounts may have a negative effect on your score. in addition, many scoring systems consider the type of credit accounts you have. For example, under some scoring models, loans from finance companies may have a negative effect on your credit score

Scoring models may be based on more than the information in your credit report. When you are applying for a mortgage loan, for example, the system may consider the amount of your down payment, your total debt, and your income, among other factors. Improving your score significantly is likely to take some time, but it can be done. to improve your credit score under most systems, focus on paying your bills in a timely way, paying down any outstanding balances, and staying away from new debt.

What are my options for dealingwith debt?

Many people face a financial crisis at some point in their lives. Whether the crisis is caused by illness, the loss of a job, or overspending, it can seem overwhelming. But often, it can be overcome. Your financial situation doesn't have to go frombad to worse. If you get into financial hot water, there are options: credit counseling from a reputable organization, debt consolidation, or bankruptcy. Which path works best for you depends on your level of debt, your level of discipline, and your prospects for the future.

contact your creditors immediately if you ever have troublemaking
ends meet. tell them why it's difficult for you to pay your bills, and try to work out a modified payment plan that reduces your payments to a manageable level. don't wait until youraccounts have been turned over to a debt collector. At that point, your creditors have given up on you.

Got bad credit?
Steer clear of credit repair scams

You see the ads in newspapers, on tv, and online. You hear them on the radio. You get fliers in the mail, email messages, and maybe even calls offering credit repair services. they all make the same claims:

Credit problems? No problem!
We can remove bankruptcies, judgments, liens, and bad loans from your credit file forever!
We can erase your bad credit —100% guaranteed. Create a new credit identity — legally.

Do yourself a favor and save some money, too. don't believe These claims: they're very likely signs of a scam. indeed, attorneys at the Federal trade commission, the nation's consumer protection agency, say they've never seen a legitimate credit repair operation making those claims.

The fact is there's no quick fix for creditworthiness. No one can legally remove accurate and timely negative information from a credit report. You can improve your credit report legitimately, but it takes time, a conscious effort, and sticking to a personal debt repayment plan.

CHAPTER 2

The Fair Credit Reporting Act (FCRA) requires each of the nationwide credit reporting companies — Equifax, Experian, and TransUnion —to provide you with a free copy of your credit report, at your request, once every 12 months. The FCRA promotes the accuracy and privacy of information in the files of the nation's credit reporting companies. The Federal Trade Commission (FTC), the nation's consumer protection agency, enforces the FCRA with respect to credit reporting companies

A credit report includes information on where you live, how you pay your bills, and whether you've been sued or have filed for bankruptcy. Nationwide credit reporting companies sell the information in your report to creditors, insurers, employers, and other businesses that use it to evaluate your applications for credit, insurance, employment, or renting a home. Here are the details about your rights under the FCRA, which established the free annual credit report program.

Q: How do I order my free report?

A: The three nationwide credit reporting companies have set up a central website, a toll-free telephone number, and a mailing address through which you can order your free annual report.

To order, visit **annualcreditreport.com**, call 1-877-322-8228, or complete the Annual Credit Report Request Form and mail it to: Annual Credit Report Request Service, P.O. Box 105281, Atlanta, GA 30348- 5281. Do not contact the three nationwide credit reporting companies individually.

A Warning About "Imposter" Websites

Only one website is authorized to fill orders for the free annual credit report you are entitled to under law — annualcreditreport.com. Other websites that claim to offer "free credit reports," "free credit scores," or "free credit monitoring" are not part of the legally mandated free annual credit report program. In some cases, the "free" product comes with strings attached. For example, some sites sign you up for a supposedly "free" service that converts to one you have to pay for after a trial period.

If you don't cancel during the trial period, you may be unwittingly agreeing to let the company start charging fees to your credit card.

Some "imposter" sites use terms like "free report" in their names; others have URLsthat purposely misspell

annualcreditreport.com in the hope that you will mistype the name of the official site. Some of these "imposter" sites direct you to other sites that try to sell you something or collect your personal information.

Annualcreditreport.com and the nationwide credit reporting companies will not send you an email asking for your personal information. If you get an email, see a pop-up ad, or get a phone call from someone claiming to be from

annualcreditreport.com or any of the three nationwide credit reporting companies, do not reply or click on any link in the message. It's probably a scam.

They are providing free annual credit reports only through annualcreditreport.com, 1-877-322-8228, and Annual Credit Report Request Service, P.O. Box 105281, Atlanta, GA 30345.

You may order your reports from each of the three nationwide credit reporting companies at the same time, or you can order your report from each of the companies one at a time. The law allows you to order one free copy of your report from each of The nationwide credit reporting companies every 12 months.

Q: What information do I need to provide to get my freereport?

A: You need to provide your name, address, Social Security number, and date of birth. If you have moved in the last two years, you may have to provide your previous address. To maintain the security of your file, each nationwide credit reporting company may ask you for some information that only you would know, like the amount of your monthly mortgage payment. Each company may ask you for different information because the information each has in your file may come from different sources.

They are providing free annual credit reports only through **annualcreditreport.com**, 1-877-322-8228, and Annual Credit Report Request Service, P.O. Box 105281, Atlanta, GA 30348-5281.

You may order your reports from each of the three nationwide credit reporting companies at the same time, or you can order your report from each of the companies one at a time. The law allows you to order one free copy of your report from each of the nationwide credit reporting companies every 12 months.

Q: How long does it take to get my report?

A: If you request your report online at annualcreditreport.com, you should be able to access it immediately. If you order your report by calling toll-free 1-877-322-8228, your report will be processed and mailed to you within 15 days. If you order your report by mail using the Annual Credit Report Request Form, your request will be processed and mailed to you within 15 days of receipt.

Whether you order your report online, by phone, or by mail, it may take longer to receive your report if the nationwide credit reporting company needs more information to verify your identity.

credit reporting company needs more information to verify your identity help guard against identity theft. That's when someone uses your personal information —like your name, your Social Security number, or your credit card number —to commit fraud. Identity thieves may use your information to open a new credit card account in your name. Then, when they don't pay the bills, the delinquent account is reported on your credit report. Inaccurate information like that could affect your ability to get credit, insurance, or even a job.

reporting company. You're also entitled to one free report a year if you're unemployed and plan to look for a job within 60 days; if you're on welfare; or if your report is inaccurate because of fraud, including identity theft. Otherwise, a credit reporting company may charge you a reasonable amount for another copy of your report within a 12-month period.

To buy a copy of your report, contact:
- Equifax:1-800-685-1111; equifax.com
- Experian: 1-888-397-3742; experian.com
- TransUnion: 1-800-916-8800; transunion.com

Q: Should I order a report from each of the three nationwide credit reporting companies?

A: It's up to you. Because nationwide credit reporting companies get their information from different sources, the information in your report from one company may not reflect all, or the same, information in your reports from the other two companies. That's not to say that the information in any of your reports is necessarily inaccurate; it just may be different.

Q: Should I order my reports from all three of the nationwide credit reporting companies at the sametime?

A: You may order one, two, or all three reports at the same time, or you may stagger your requests. It's your choice. Some financial advisors say staggering your requests during a 12-month period may be a good way to keep an eye on the accuracy and completeness of the information in your reports.

Credit cards can help

Control your Score

Q: What if I find errors —either inaccuracies or incomplete information —in my credit report?

A: Under the FCRA, both the credit reporting company and the information provider (that is, the person, company, or organization that provides information about you to a credit reporting company) are responsible for correcting inaccurate or incomplete information in your report. To take full advantage of your rights under this law, contact the credit reporting company and the information provider.

1. Tell the credit reporting company, in writing, what information you think is inaccurate.

   Credit reporting companies must investigate the items in question —usually within 30 days —unless they consider your dispute frivolous. They also must forward all the relevant data you provide about the inaccuracy to the organization that provided the information. After the information provider receives notice of a dispute from the credit reporting company, it must investigate, review the relevant information, and report the results back to the credit reporting company.

If the information provider finds the disputed information is inaccurate, it must notify all three nationwide credit reporting companies so they can correct the information in your file.

When the investigation is complete, the credit reporting company must give you the written results and a free copy of your report if the dispute results in a change. (This free report does not count as your annual free report.) If an item is changed or deleted, the credit reporting company cannot put the disputed information back in your file unless the information provider verifies that it is accurate and complete. The credit reporting company also must send you written notice that includes the name, address, and phone number of the information provider.

2. Tell the creditor or other information provider in writing that you dispute an item. Many providers specify an address for disputes. If the provider reports the item to a credit reporting company, it must include a notice of your dispute. And if you are correct —that is, if the information is found to be inaccurate —the information provider may not report it again

Q: What can I do if the credit reporting company or information provider won't correct the information I dispute?

A: If an investigation doesn't resolve your dispute with the credit reporting company, you can ask that a statement of the dispute be included in your file and in future reports.

You also can ask the credit reporting company to provide your statement to anyone who received a copy of your report in the recent past. You can expect to pay a fee for this service.

If you tell the information provider that you dispute an item, a notice of your dispute must be included any time the information provider reports the item to a credit reporting company.

Q: How long can a credit reporting company report negative information?

A: A credit reporting company can report most accurate negative information for seven years and bankruptcy information for 10 years. There is no time limit on reporting information about criminal convictions;

information reported in response to your application for a job that pays more than $75,000 a year; and information reported because you've applied for more than $150,000 worth of credit or life insurance. Information about a lawsuit or an unpaid judgment against you can be reported for seven years or until the statute of limitations runs out, whichever is longer.

Q: Can anyone else get a copy of my credit report?

A: The FCRA specifies who can access your credit report. Creditors, insurers, employers, and other businesses that use the information in your report to evaluate your applications for credit, insurance, employment, or renting a home are among those that have a legal right to access your report.

Q: Can my employer get my credit report? A: Your employer can get a copy of your credit report only if you agree. A credit reporting company may not provide information about you to your employer, or to a prospective employer, without your written consent.

CHAPTER 3

You hear them on the radio. You get fliers in the mail, email messages, and maybe even calls offering credit repair services. They all make the same claims:

"Credit problems? No problem!"

"We can remove bankruptcies, judgments, liens, and bad loans from your credit file forever!"

"We can erase your bad credit — 100% guaranteed."

"Create a new credit identity — legally."

Do yourself a favor and save some money, too. Don't believe these claims: they're very likely signs of a scam. Indeed, attorneys at the Federal Trade Commission, the nation's consumer protection agency, say they've never seen a legitimate credit repair operation making those claims. The fact is there's no Quick fix for creditworthiness. You can improve your credit report legitimately, but it takes time, a conscious effort, and sticking to a personal debt repayment plan.

Your Rights

No one can legally remove accurate and timely negative information from a credit report. You can ask for an investigation at no charge to you for information in your file that you dispute as inaccurate or incomplete. Some people hire a company to investigate for them, but anything a credit repair company can do legally, you can do for yourself at little or no cost.

By law:

You're entitled to a free credit report if a company takes "adverse action" against you, like denying your application for credit, insurance, or employment. You have to ask for your report within 60 days of receiving notice of the action.

The notice includes the name, address, and phone number of the consumer reporting company. You're also entitled to one free report a year if you're unemployed and plan to look for a job within 60 days; if you're on welfare; or if your report is inaccurate because of fraud, including identity theft.

- Each of the nationwide credit reporting companies —Equifax, Experian, and TransUnion —is required to provide you with a free copy of your credit report once every 12 months, if you ask for it. To order, visit **annualcreditreport.com**, call 1-877-322-8228, or use the form at the center of this booklet. You may order reports from each of the three credit reporting companies at the same time, or you can stagger your requests throughout the year.

It doesn't cost anything to dispute mistakes or outdated items on your credit report. Both the credit reporting company and the information provider (the person, company, or organization that provides information about you to a credit reporting Company) are responsible for correcting inaccurate or Incomplete information in your report. To take advantage of all your rights, contact both the credit reporting company and the information provider.

DIY

Step 1: Tell the credit reporting company, in writing, what information you think is inaccurate. Include copies (NOT originals) of any documents that support your position. In addition to including your complete name and address, your letter should identify each item in your report that you dispute; state the facts and the reasons you dispute the Information, and ask that it be removed or corrected. You may want to enclose a copy of your report, and circle the items in question.

Send your letter by certified mail, "return receipt requested," so you can document that the credit reporting company got it. Keep copies of your dispute letter and enclosures.

Credit reporting companies must investigate the items you question within 30 days —unless they consider your dispute frivolous. They must forward all the relevant data you provide about the inaccuracy to the organization that provided the information. After the information provider gets notice of a dispute from the credit reporting company, it must investigate, review the relevant information, and report the results back to the credit reporting company.

If the investigation reveals that the disputed information is inaccurate, the information provider has to notify the nationwide credit reporting companies so they can correct it in your file. When the investigation is complete, the credit reporting company must give you the results in writing, too, and a free copy of your report if the dispute results in a change. If an item is changed or deleted, the credit reporting company cannot put the disputed Information back in your file unless the information provider verifies that it's accurate and complete. The credit reporting company also must send you written notice that includes the name, address, and phone number of the information provider. If you ask, the credit reporting company must send notices of any correction to anyone who got your report in the past six months. You also can ask that a corrected copy of your report be sent to anyone who got a copy during the past two years for employment purposes. If an investigation doesn't resolve your dispute with the credit reporting company, you can ask that a statement of the dispute be included in your file and in future reports. You also can ask the credit reporting company to give your statement to anyone who got a copy of your report in the recent past. You'll probably have to pay for this service.

Step 2: Tell the creditor or other information provider, in writing, that you dispute an item. Include copies (NOT originals) of documents that support your position. Many providers specify an address for disputes. If the provider reports the item to a consumer reporting company, it must include a notice of your dispute. And if the information is found to be inaccurate, the provider may not report it again.

Date

Your Name
Your Address
City, State, Zip Code

Sample Letter
Use this sample letter to help write your own.

Complaint Department Name of
Company Address
City, State, Zip Code

Dear Sir or Madam:

I am writing to dispute the following information in my file. The items I dispute also are circled on the attached copy of the report I received.

This item (identify item(s) disputed by name of source, such as creditors or tax court, and identify type of item, such as credit account, judgment, etc.) is (inaccurate or incomplete) because (describe what is inaccurate or incomplete and why). I am requesting that the item be deleted (or request another specific change) to correct the information.

Enclosed are copies of (use this sentence if applicable and describe any enclosed documentation, such as payment records, court documents) supporting my position. Please investigate this (these) matter(s) and (delete or correct) the disputed item(s) as soon as possible.

Sincerely, Your name

Call Equifax for information

Call Transunion for information

Reporting Accurate Negative Information

When negative information in your report is accurate, only time can make it go away. A credit reporting company can report most accurate negative information for seven years and bankruptcy information for 10 years. Information about an unpaid judgment against you can be reported for seven years or until the statute of limitations runs out, whichever is longer. The seven-year reporting period starts from the date the event took place. There is no time limit on reporting information about criminal convictions; information reported in response to your application for a job that pays more than $75,000 a year; and information reported because you've applied for more than $150,000 worth of credit or life insurance.

The Credit Repair Organizations Act

The Credit Repair Organization Act (CROA) makes it illegal for credit repair companies to lie about what they can do for you, and to charge you before they've performed their services. The CROA is enforced by the Federal Trade Commission and requires credit repair companies to explain:

- your legal rights in a written contract that also details the services they'll perform
- your three day right to cancel without any charge
- how long it will take to get results
- the total cost you will pay
- any guarantees

What if a credit repair company you hired doesn't live up to its promises? You have some options. You can:

- sue them in federal court for your actual losses or for what you paid them, whichever is more
- seek punitive damages —money to punish the company for violating the law
- join other people in a class action lawsuit against the company, and if you win, the company has to pay your attorney's fees

Report Credit Repair Fraud

State Attorneys General

Many states also have laws regulating credit repair companies. If you have a problem with a credit repair company, report it to your local consumer affairs office or to your state attorney general (AG, **www.naag.org**).

If you're not disciplined enough to create a budget and stick to it, to work out a repayment plan with your creditors, or to keep track of your mounting bills, you might consider contacting a credit counseling organization. Many are nonprofit and work with you to solve your financial problems. But remember that

problems. But remember that "nonprofit" status doesn't

guarantee free, affordable, or even legitimate services. In fact, some credit counseling organizations —even some that claim nonprofit status may charge high fees or hide their fees by pressuring people to make "voluntary" contributions that only cause more debt.

Most credit counselors offer services through local offices, online, or on the phone. If possible, find an organization that offers in-person counseling. Many universities, military bases, credit unions, housing authorities, and branches of the U.S. Cooperative Extension Service operate nonprofit credit counseling programs. Your financial institution, local consumer protection agency, and friends and family also may be good sources of information and referrals.

Most credit counselors offer services through local offices, online, or on the phone. If possible, find an organization that offers in-person counseling. Many universities, military bases, credit unions, housing authorities, and branches of the U.S. Cooperative Extension Service operate nonprofit credit counseling programs. Your financial institution, local consumer protection agency, and friends and family also may be good sources of information and referrals.

Where to Get Legitimate Help

Just because you have a poor credit history doesn't mean you can't get credit. Creditors set their own standards, and not all look at your credit history the same way. Some may look only at recent years to evaluate you for credit, and they may give you credit if your bill-paying history has improved. It may be worthwhile to contact creditors informally to discuss their credit standards

If you're thinking about filing for bankruptcy, be aware that bankruptcy laws require that you get credit counseling from a government-approved organization within six months before you file for bankruptcy relief. You can find a state-by-state list of government-approved organizations at www.usdoj.gov/ust, the website of the U.S. Trustee Program. That's the organization within the U.S. Department of Justice that supervises bankruptcy cases and trustees. Be wary of credit counseling organizations that say they are government-approved, but don't appear on the list of approved organizations.

Reputable credit counseling organizations can advise you on managing your money and debts, help you develop a budget, and offer free educational materials and workshops. Their counselors are certified and trained in the areas of consumer credit, money and debt management, and budgeting. Counselors discuss your entire financial situation with you, and can help you develop a personalized plan to solve your money problems. An initial counseling session typically lasts an hour, with an offer of follow-up sessions.

Applications for credit, insurance, employment, and even leases. They can use it when they choose to give or deny you credit or insurance, provided you receive fair and equal treatment.

CHAPTER 4

The Federal Trade Commission (FTC) enforces the credit laws that protect your right to get, use and maintain credit. These laws do not guarantee that everyone will receive credit. Instead, the credit laws protect your rights by requiring businesses to give all consumers a fair and equal opportunity to get credit and to resolve disputes over credit errors. This brochure explains your rights under these laws and offers practical tips to help you solve credit problems.

The Federal Trade Commission (FTC) enforces the credit laws that protect your right to get, use and maintain credit. These laws do not guarantee that everyone will receive credit. Instead, the credit laws protect your rights by requiring businesses to give all consumers a fair and equal opportunity to get credit and to resolve disputes over credit errors. This brochure explains your rights under these laws and offers practical tips to help you solve credit problems.

Under the Fair Credit Reporting Act:

▶ You have the right to receive a copy of your credit report. The copy of your report must contain all the information in your file at the time of your request.

▶ Each of the nationwide credit reporting companies – Equifax, Experian, and TransUnion – is required to provide you with a free copy of your credit report, at your request, once every 12 months.

▶ Under federal law, you're also entitled to a free report if a company takes adverse action against you, like denying your application for credit, insurance, or employment, and you ask for your report within 60 days of receiving notice of the action. The notice will give you the name, address, and phone number of the credit reporting company. You're also entitled to one free report a year if you're unemployed and plan to look for a job within 60 days; if you're on welfare; or if your report is inaccurate because of fraud, including identity theft.

Your Credit Application

When creditors evaluate a credit application, they cannot engage in discriminatory practices.

The **Equal Credit Opportunity Act (ECOA)** prohibits credit discrimination on the basis of sex, race, marital status, religion, national origin, age, or receipt of public assistance. Creditors may ask for this information (except religion) in certain situations, but they may not use it to discriminate against you when deciding whether to grant you credit.

The ECOA protects consumers who deal with companies that regularly extend credit, including banks, small loan and finance companies, retail and department stores, credit card companies, and credit unions. Everyone who participates in the decision to grant credit, including real estate brokers who arrange financing, must follow this law. Businesses applying for credit also are protected by this law. Under the Equal Credit Opportunity Act:

- ▶ You cannot be denied credit based on your race, sex, marital status, religion, age, national origin, or receipt of public assistance.
- ▶ You have the right to have reliable public assistance considered in the same manner as other income.
- ▶ If you are denied credit, you have a legal right to know why.

Your Credit Billing and Electronic Fund Transfer Statements

It is important to check credit billing and electronic fund transfer account statements regularly because these documents may contain mistakes that could damage your credit status or reflect improper charges or transfers. If you find an error or discrepancy, notify the company and dispute the error immediately. The **Fair Credit Billing Act (FCBA)** and **Electronic Fund Transfer Act (EFTA)** establish procedures for resolving mistakes on credit billing and electronic fund transfer account statements, including:

- ▶ charges or electronic fund transfers that you – or anyone you have authorized to use your account – have not made;
- ▶ charges or electronic fund transfers that are incorrectly identified or show the wrong date or amount;
- ▶ math errors;
- ▶ failure to post payments, credits, or electronic fund transfers properly;
- ▶ failure to send bills to your current address – provided the creditor receives your change of address, in writing, at least 20 days before the billing period ends;
- ▶ charges or electronic fund transfers for which you ask for an explanation or written proof of

purchase along with a claimed error or request for clarification.

The FCBA generally applies only to "open end" credit accounts – credit cards and revolving charge accounts, like department store accounts. It does not apply to loans or credit sales that are paid according to a fixed schedule until the entire amount is paid back, like an automobile loan. The EFTA applies to electronic fund transfers, like those involving automatic teller machines (ATMs), point- of-sale debit transactions, and other electronic banking transactions.

Your Debts and Debt Collectors

You are responsible for your debts. If you fall behind in paying your creditors, or if an error is made on your account, you may be contacted by a "debt collector." A debt collector is any person, other than the creditor, who regularly collects debts owed to others, including lawyers who collect debts on a regular basis. You have the right to be treated fairly by debt collectors.

The **Fair Debt Collection Practices Act (FDCPA)** applies to personal, family, and household debts. This includes money you owe for the purchase of a car, for medical care, or for charge accounts. The FDCPA prohibits debt collectors from engaging in unfair, deceptive, or abusive practices while collecting these debts. Under the FDCPA:

▶ Debt collectors may contact you only between 8 a.m. and 9 p.m.

▶ Debt collectors may not contact you at work if they know your employer disapproves.

▶ Debt collectors may not harass, oppress, or abuse you.

- Debt collectors may not lie when collecting debts, such as falsely implying that you have committed a crime.

- Debt collectors must identify themselves to you on the phone.

- Debt collectors must stop contacting you if you ask them to do so in writing.

Solving Your Credit Problems

Your credit report can influence your purchasing power, as well as your opportunity to get a job, rent or buy an apartment or a house, and buy insurance. When negative information in your report is accurate, only the passage of time can assure its removal. A credit reporting company can report most accurate negative information for seven years and bankruptcy information for 10 years.

Information about an unpaid judgment against you can be reported for seven years or until the statute of limitations runs out, whichever is longer. There is no time limit on reporting information about criminal convictions; information reported in response to your application for a job that pays more than $75,000 a year; and information reported because you've applied for more than $150,000 worth of credit or life insurance. There is a standard method for calculating the seven-year reporting period. Generally, the period runs from the date that the event took place.

▶ If in doubt, request written verification of a debt.

▶ Keep all your original documents, especially receipts, sales slips, and billing statements. You will need them if you dispute a credit bill or report. Send copies only. It may take more than one letter to correct a problem.

▶ Be skeptical of businesses that offer instant solutions to credit problems: There aren't any.

▶ Be persistent. Resolving credit problems can take time and patience.

▶ There is nothing that a credit repair company can charge you for that you cannot do for yourself for little or no cost.

If you're not disciplined enough to create a workable budget and stick to it, work out a repayment plan with your creditors, or keep track of mounting bills, consider contacting a credit counseling organization. Many credit counseling organizations are nonprofit and work with you to solve your financial problems. But not all are reputable. For example, just because an organization says it's "nonprofit," there's no guarantee that its services are free, affordable, or even legitimate. In fact, some credit counseling organizations charge high fees, or hide their fees by pressuring consumers to make "voluntary" contributions that only cause more debt.

Most credit counselors offer services through local offices, the Internet, or on the telephone. If possible, find an organization that offers in-person counseling. Many universities, military bases, credit unions, Housing

authorities, and branches of the U.S. Cooperative Extension Service operate nonprofit credit counseling programs. Your financial institution, local consumer protection agency, and friends and family also may be good sources of information and referrals.

Reputable credit counseling organizations can advise you on managing your money and debts, help you develop a budget, and offer free educational materials and workshops. Their counselors are certified and trained in the areas of consumer credit, money and debt management, and budgeting. Counselors discuss your entire financial situation with you, and help you develop a personalized plan to solve your money problems. An initial counseling session typically lasts an hour, with an offer of follow-up sessions.

CHAPTER 5

Y where you live, how you pay your bills, and whether you've been sued or arrested, or have filed for bankruptcy. Credit reporting companies sell the information in your report to creditors, insurers, employers, and other businesses that use it to evaluate your applications for credit, insurance, employment, or renting a home.

The federal Fair Credit Reporting Act (FCRA) promotes the accuracy and privacy of information in the files of the nation's credit reporting companies.

Some financial advisors and consumer advocates suggest that you review your credit report periodically. Why?

- Because the information it contains affects whether you can get a loan —and how much you will have to pay to borrow money.

- To make sure the information is accurate, complete, and up-to-date before you apply for a loan for a major purchase like a house or car, buy insurance, or apply for a job.

- To help guard against identity theft. That's when someone uses your personal information —like your name, your Social Security number, or your credit card number —to commit fraud. Identity thieves may use your information to open a new credit card account in your name. Then, when they don't pay the bills, the delinquent account is reported on your credit report. Inaccurate information like that could affect your ability to get credit, insurance, or even a job.

How to Order Your Free Report

An amendment to the FCRA requires each of the nationwide credit reporting companies —Equifax, Experian, and TransUnion —to provide you with a free copy of your credit report, at your request, once every 12 months.

The three nationwide credit reporting companies have set up one website, toll-free telephone number, and mailing address through which you can order your free annual report. To order, visit **annualcreditreport.com**, call 1-877-322-8228, or complete the Annual Credit Report Request Form at the center of this booklet and mail it to:

Annual Credit Report Request Service

P.O. Box 105281
Atlanta, GA 30348-5281

Do not contact the three nationwide credit reporting companies individually.

Do not contact the three nationwide credit reporting companies individually.

You may order your reports from each of the three nationwide credit reporting companies at the same time, or you can order from only one or two. The FCRA allows you to order one free copy from each of the nationwide credit reporting companies every 12 months.

You need to provide your name, address, Social Security number, and date of birth. If you have moved in the last two years, you may have to provide your previous address. To maintain the security of your file, each nationwide credit reporting company

You're also entitled to one free report a year if you're unemployed and plan to look for a job within 60 days; if you're on welfare; or if your report is inaccurate because of fraud, including identity theft.

Otherwise, a credit reporting company may charge you a reasonable amount for another copy of your report within a 12-month period. To buy a copy of your report, contact the three credit report companies:

Experian-1-888-397-3742 www.experian.com
TransUnion-1-800-916-8800 www.transunion.com

Equifax-1-800-685-1111 www.equifax.com

may ask you for some information that only you would know, like the amount of your monthly mortgage payment. Each company may ask you for different information because the information each has in your file may come from different sources.

Other situations where you might be eligible for a free report

You're also entitled to a free report if a company takes adverse action against you, such as denying your application for credit, insurance, or employment, based on information in your report. You must ask for your report within 60 days of receiving notice of the action. The notice will give you the name, address, and phone number of the credit reporting company.

Correcting Errors

Under the FCRA, both the credit reporting company and the information provider (that is, the person, company, or organization that provides information about you to a credit reporting company) are responsible for correcting inaccurate or incomplete information in your report. To take advantage of all your rights under this law, contact the credit reporting company and the information provider.

Step One

Tell the credit reporting company, in writing, what information you think is inaccurate. Include copies (NOT originals) of documents that support your position. In addition to providing your complete name and address, your letter should clearly identify each item in your report you dispute, state the facts and explain why you dispute the information, and request that it be removed or corrected

You may want to enclose a copy of your report with the items in question circled. Your letter may look something like the one below. Send your letter by certified mail, "return receipt requested," so you can document what the credit reporting company received. Keep copies of your dispute letter and enclosures.

Credit reporting companies must investigate the items in question —usually within 30 days —unless they consider your dispute frivolous. They also must forward all the relevant data you provide about the inaccuracy to the organization that provided the information. After the information provider Receives notice of a dispute from the credit reporting company, it must investigate, review the relevant information, and report the results back to the credit reporting company. If the information provider finds the disputed information is inaccurate, it must notify all three nationwide credit reporting companies so they can correct the information in your file.

When the investigation is complete, the credit reporting company must give you the results in writing and a free copy of your report if the dispute results in a change. This free report does not count as your annual free report. If an item is changed or deleted, the credit reporting company cannot put the disputed information back in your file unless the information provider verifies that it is accurate and complete. The credit reporting company also must send you written notice that includes the name, address, and phone number of the information provider.

If you ask, the credit reporting company must send notices of any corrections to anyone who received your report in the past six months. You can have a corrected copy of your report sent to anyone who received a copy during the past two years for employment purposes.

If an investigation doesn't resolve your dispute with the credit reporting company, you can ask that a statement of the dispute be included in your file and in future reports. You also can ask the credit reporting company to provide your statement to anyone who received a copy of your report in the recent past. You can expect to pay a fee for this service.

Step Two

Tell the information provider (that is, the person, company, or organization that provides information about you to a credit reporting company), in writing, that you dispute an item in your credit report. Use the sample dispute letter on page 10. Include copies (NOT originals) of documents that support your position. If the provider listed an address on your credit report, send your letter to that address. If no

address is listed, contact the provider and ask for the correct address to send your letter. If the information provider does not give you an address, you can send your letter to any business address for that provider.

If the provider continues to report the item you dispute to a credit reporting company, it must let the credit reporting company know about your dispute. And if you are correct —that is, if the information you dispute is found to be inaccurate or incomplete — the information provider must tell the credit reporting company to update or delete the item.

If the provider continues to report the item you dispute to a credit reporting company, it must let the credit reporting company know about your dispute. And if you are correct —that is, if the information you dispute is found to be inaccurate or incomplete — the information provider must tell the credit reporting company to update or delete the item.

About Your File

Your credit file may not reflect all your credit accounts.

Although most national department store and all-purpose bank credit card accounts will be included in your file, not all creditors supply information to credit reporting companies: some local retailers, credit unions, travel, entertainment, and gasoline card companies are among the creditors that don't.

When negative information in your report is accurate, only the passage of time can assure its removal. A credit reporting company can report most accurate negative information for seven years and bankruptcy information for 10 years. Information about an unpaid judgment against you can be reported for seven years or until the statute of limitations runs out, whichever is longer. There is no time limit on reporting: information about criminal convictions; information reported in response to your application for a job that pays more than $75,000 a year; and

information reported because you've applied for more than $150,000 worth of credit or life insurance. There is a standard method for calculating the seven-year reporting period. Generally, the period runs from the date that the event took place.

[Your Name] [Your Address] **Sample Dispute Letter**
[Your City, State, Zip Code]

[Date]

Complaint Department [Company Name] [Street Address]
[City, State, Zip Code]

Dear Sir or Madam:

I am writing to dispute the following information in my file. I have circled the items I dispute on the attached copy of the report I received.

This item [identify item(s) disputed by name of source, such as creditors or tax court, and identify type of item, such as credit account, judgment, etc.] is [inaccurate or incomplete] because [describe what is inaccurate or incomplete and why]. I am requesting that the item be removed [or request another specific change] to correct the information.

Enclosed are copies of [use this sentence if applicable and describe any enclosed documentation, such as payment records and court documents] supporting my position.
Please reinvestigate this [these] matter[s] and [delete or correct] the disputed item[s] as soon as possible.

Sincerely, Your name

Enclosures: [List what you are enclosing.]

Know Your Credit Score

A Good Credit Score means Savings for you

CHAPTER 6

The Federal Trade Commission (FTC), the nation's consumer protection agency, enforces the Equal Credit Opportunity Act (ECOA), which prohibits credit discrimination on the basis of race, color, religion, national origin, sex, marital status, age, or because you get public assistance. Creditors may ask you for most of this information in certain situations, but they may not use it when deciding whether to give you credit or when setting the terms of your credit. Not everyone who applies for credit gets it or gets the same terms: Factors like income, expenses, debts, and credit history are among the considerations lenders use to determine your creditworthiness.

The law provides protections when you deal with any organizations or people who regularly extend credit, including banks, small loan and finance companies, retail and department stores, credit card companies, and credit unions. Everyone who participates in the decision to grant credit or in setting the terms of that credit, including real estate brokers who arrange financing, must comply with the ECOA.

When You Apply For Credit, Creditors May Not...

- Discourage you from applying or reject your application because of your race, color, religion, national origin, sex, marital status, age, or because you receive public assistance.

- Consider your race, sex, or national origin, although you may be asked to disclose this information if you want to. It helps federal agencies enforce anti-discrimination laws. A creditor may consider your immigration status and whether you have the right to stay in the country long enough to repay the debt.

- Impose different terms or conditions, like a higher interest rate or higher fees, on a loan based on your race, color, religion, national origin, sex, marital status, age, or because you receive public assistance.

- Ask if you're widowed or divorced. A creditor may use only the terms: married, unmarried, or separated.

- Ask about your marital status if you're applying for a separate, unsecured account. A creditor may ask you to provide this information if you live in "community property" states: Arizona, California, Idaho, Louisiana, Nevada, New Mexico, Texas, Washington, and Wisconsin. A creditor in any state may ask for this information if you apply for a joint account or one secured by property.

- Ask for information about your spouse, except:
  - if your spouse is applying with you;
  - if your spouse will be allowed to use the account;
  - if you are relying on your spouse's income or on alimony or child support income from a former spouse;

♦ if you live in a community property state.

- Ask about your plans for having or raising children, but they can ask questions about expenses related to your dependents.

- Ask if you get alimony, child support, or separate maintenance payments, unless they tell you first that you don't have to provide this information if you aren't relying on these payments to get credit. A creditor may ask if you have to pay alimony, child support, or separate maintenance payments.

When Deciding To Grant You Credit Or When Setting The Terms Of Credit, Creditors May Not...

- Consider your race, color, religion, national origin, sex, marital status or whether you get public assistance.

- Consider your age, unless:

  - you're too young to sign contracts, generally under 18;

  - you're at least 62, and the creditor will favor you because of your age;

  - it's used to determine the meaning of other factors important to creditworthiness. For example, a creditor could use your age to determine if your income might drop because you're about to retire;

It's used in a valid credit scoring system that favors applicants 62 and older. A credit scoring system assigns points to answers you give on credit applications. For example, your length of employment might be scored differently depending on your age.

- Consider whether you have a telephone account in your name. A creditor may consider whether you have a phone.

- Consider the racial composition of the neighborhood where you want to buy, refinance or improve a house with money you are borrowing.

When Evaluating Your Income, Creditors May Not...

- Refuse to consider reliable public assistance income the same way as other income.

- Discount income because of your sex or marital status. For example, a creditor cannot count a man's salary at 100 percent and a woman's at 75 percent. A creditor may not assume a woman of childbearing age will stop working to raise children.

- Discount or refuse to consider income because it comes from part-time employment, Social Security, pensions, or annuities.

- Refuse to consider reliable alimony, child support, or separate maintenance payments. A creditor may ask you for proof that you receive this income consistently.

You Also Have The Right To...

- Have credit in your birth name (Mary Smith), your first and your spouse's last name (Mary Jones), or your first name and a combined last name (Mary Smith Jones).

- Get credit without a cosigner, if you meet the creditor's standards.

- Have a cosigner other than your spouse, if one is necessary.

- Keep your own accounts after you change your name, marital status, reach a certain age, or retire, unless the creditor has evidence that you're not willing or able to pay.

- Know whether your application was accepted or rejected within 30 days of filing a complete application.

- Know why your application was rejected. The creditor must tell you the specific reason for the rejection or that you are entitled to learn the reason if you ask within 60 days. An acceptable reason might be: "your income was too low" or "you haven't been employed long enough." An unacceptable reason might be "you didn't meet our minimum standards." That information isn't specific enough.

- Learn the specific reason you were offered less favorable terms than you applied for, but only if you reject these terms. For example, if the lender offers you a smaller loan or a higher interest rate, and you don't accept the offer, you have the right to know why those terms were offered.

- Learn the specific reason you were offered less favorable terms than you applied for, but only if you reject these terms. For example, if the lender offers you a smaller loan or a higher interest rate, and you don't accept the offer, you have the right to know why those terms were offered.

- Find out why your account was closed or why the terms of the account were made less favorable, unless the account was inactive or you failed to make payments as agreed.

A Special Note To Women

A good credit history — a record of your bill payments — often is necessary to get credit. This can hurt many married, separated, divorced, and widowed women. Typically, there are two reasons women don't have credit histories in their own names: either they lost their credit histories when they married and changed their names, or creditors reported accounts shared by married couples in the husband's name only.

A Special Note To Women Continued...

If you're married, separated, divorced, or widowed, contact your Local credit reporting companies to make sure all relevant bill payment information is in a file under your own name. Your credit report includes information on where you live, how you pay your bills, and whether you've been sued, arrested or filed for bankruptcy. National credit reporting companies sell the information in your report to creditors, insurers, employers, and other businesses that, in turn, use it to evaluate your applications for credit, insurance, employment, or renting a home

If You Suspect a Creditor has Discriminated Against You, Take Action

- Complain to the creditor. Sometimes you can persuade the creditor to reconsider your application.

- Check with your state Attorney General's office (naag.org) to see if the creditor violated state equal credit opportunity laws.

- Consider suing the creditor in federal district court. If you win, you can recover your actual damages and be awarded punitive damages if the court finds that the creditor's conduct was willful. You also may recover reasonable lawyers' fees and court costs. Or you might consider finding others with the same claim, and getting together to file a class action suit. An attorney can advise you on how to proceed.

If You Suspect a Creditor has Discriminated Against You, Take Action

- Complain to the creditor. Sometimes you can persuade the creditor to reconsider your application.

- Check with your state Attorney General's office (naag.org) to see if the creditor violated state equal credit opportunity laws.

- Consider suing the creditor in federal district court. If you win, you can recover your actual damages and be awarded punitive damages if the court finds that the creditor's conduct was willful. You also may recover reasonable lawyers' fees and court costs. Or you might consider finding others with the same claim, and getting together to file a class action suit. An attorney can advise you on how to proceed.

- Report violations to the appropriate government agency. If you've been denied credit, the creditor must give you the name and address of the agency to contact.

Disclaimer Statement

All information and content contained in this book are provided solely for general information and reference purposes. Smith Show Publishing LLC Limited makes no statement, representation, warranty or guarantee as to the accuracy, reliability or timeliness of the information and content contained in this Book.

Neither Smith Show Publishing Limited or the author of this book nor any of its related company accepts any responsibility or liability for any direct or indirect loss or damage (whether in tort, contract or otherwise) which may be suffered or occasioned by any person howsoever arising due to any inaccuracy, omission, misrepresentation or error in respect of any information and content provided by this book (including any third-party books.

SSP

www.ingramcontent.com/pod-product-compliance
Lightning Source LLC
Chambersburg PA
CBHW081752100526
44592CB00015B/2400